OCT 3 1 2019

Cool Careers
in Science

▸ Designing
rollercoasters,
waterparks,
and more

▸ Key skills for
success

▸ Learn how
to become one

ENTERTAINMENT
Engineers

ALTERNATIVE REALITY DEVELOPERS

ARTIFICIAL INTELLIGENCE SCIENTISTS

COMPUTER GAME & APP DEVELOPERS

DRIVERLESS VEHICLE DEVELOPERS

DRONE PILOTS

ENTERTAINMENT ENGINEERS

FORENSIC SCIENTISTS

PROFESSIONAL HACKERS

RENEWABLE ENERGY WORKERS

ROBOTICS DEVELOPERS

Cool Careers in Science

ENTERTAINMENT
Engineers

ANDREW MORKES

MASON CREST
PHILADELPHIA
MIAMI

Mason Crest
450 Parkway Drive, Suite D
Broomall, Pennsylvania 19008
(866) MCP-BOOK (toll-free)

First printing

9 8 7 6 5 4 3 2 1

HARDBACK ISBN: 978-1-4222-4298-8
SERIES ISBN: 978-1-4222-4292-6
E-BOOK ISBN: 978-1-4222-7515-3

Cataloging-in-Publication Data on file with the Library of Congress

Developed and Produced by National Highlights, Inc.
Interior and cover design: Jana Rade, impact studios
Interior layout: Annalisa Gumbrecht, Studio Gumbrecht
Production: Michelle Luke
Proofreader: Susan Uttendorfsky

QR CODES AND LINKS TO THIRD-PARTY CONTENT

Table of Contents

KEY ICONS TO LOOK FOR:

 WORDS TO UNDERSTAND: These words with their easy-to-understand definitions will increase the reader's understanding of the text while building vocabulary skills.

 SIDEBARS: This boxed material within the main text allows readers to build knowledge, gain insights, explore possibilities, and broaden their perspectives by weaving together additional information to provide realistic and holistic perspectives.

 EDUCATIONAL VIDEOS: Readers can view videos by scanning our QR codes, providing them with additional educational content to supplement the text. Examples include news coverage, moments in history, speeches, iconic sports moments, and much more!

TEXT-DEPENDENT QUESTIONS: These questions send the reader back to the text for more careful attention to the evidence presented there.

 RESEARCH PROJECTS: Readers are pointed toward areas of further inquiry connected to each chapter. Suggestions are provided for projects that encourage deeper research and analysis.

CAREERS IN SCIENCE OFFER GOOD PAY, THE OPPORTUNITY TO HELP PEOPLE, AND OTHER REWARDS

Where would we be without science? Well, we'd be without computers, smartphones, and other cutting-edge technologies. Crimes would take longer to solve without modern forensic analysis techniques. We'd be stuck relying on environmentally unfriendly fossil fuels instead of using renewable energy. And life would be less fun because we wouldn't have drones, awe-inspiring and physics-defying roller coasters, and the computer and video games that we play for hours.

Job markets are sometimes strong and sometimes weak, but a career in science (which, for the purposes of this series, includes the related fields of technology and engineering) is almost a sure path to a comfortable life. The following paragraphs provide more information on why a career in science is a great choice.

Good pay. People in science careers earn some of the highest salaries in the work world. The median annual salary for those in engineering careers in the United States is $79,180, according to the U.S. Department of Labor (USDL). This is much higher than the median earnings ($37,690) for all careers. Additionally, those in life, physical, and social science occupations earn $64,510. Science professionals who become managers or who launch their own businesses can earn anywhere from $150,000 to $300,000 or more.

Strong employment prospects. There are shortages of science workers throughout the world, according to the consulting firm ManpowerGroup. In fact, engineering workers are the third most in-demand occupational field in the world. Technicians rank fourth, and computer and information technology professionals rank sixth.

There's a shortage of software engineers in more than twenty countries, including the United States, Canada, Mexico, Japan, and the United Kingdom, according to the recruitment firm Michael Page. Other science careers where there is a shortage of workers include electronics engineers (nineteen countries), electrical engineers (sixteen countries), data analysts (eleven countries), and hardware engineers (six countries).

The USDL predicts that employment of computer and information technology professionals in the United States will grow by 13 percent during the next decade. Career opportunities for those in life, physical, and social science occupations will grow by 10 percent. Both of these occupational fields are growing faster than the average for all careers.

The outlook is also good for engineering professionals. Employment is expected to grow by 7 percent during the next decade. The strongest opportunities will be found in renewable energy and robotics.

By 2026, the USDL predicts that there will be more than 876,000 new jobs in science, technology, engineering, and mathematics fields.

Rewarding work environment and many career options. A career in science is fulfilling because you get to use both your creative and practical sides to develop new technologies (or improve existing ones), solve problems, and make the world a better place. In the instance of entertainment engineering, you get the chance to make the world a more fun place! There's a common misconception that science workers spend most of their time in dreary, windowless laboratories or research facilities. While they do spend lots of time in these places, they also spend time in the field, testing, troubleshooting, and trying out their inventions or discoveries. In the entertainment sector, engineers spend a good portion of their workday in the field, overseeing the construction, testing, and troubleshooting of new roller coasters, Ferris wheels, and other crowd-pleasing rides and facilities. Some science professionals launch their own businesses, which can be both fun and very rewarding.

IS A CAREER IN SCIENCE RIGHT FOR ME?

Test your interest. How many of these statements do you agree with?

____ My favorite class in school is science.

____ I also enjoy computer science classes.

____ I like to learn about scientific breakthroughs.

____ I like to design and build things.

____ I like to solve puzzles.

____ I enjoy doing science experiments.

____ I am curious about how things work.

____ I am creative and have a good imagination.

____ I like to build electronics and other things that require electricity.

____ I like to take things apart and see how they work.

____ I am good at math and physics.

If many of the statements above describe you, then you should consider a career in the sciences. But you don't need to select a career right now. Check out this book on a career as an entertainment engineer, and other books in the series, to learn more about occupational paths in the sciences and related fields. Good luck with your career exploration!

WORDS TO UNDERSTAND

multimedia: the use of more than one type of text, graphics, audio, and/or video to communicate or present art

sound check: a test of sound systems by musicians and audio engineers before a performance to make sure that the systems will work correctly once the event begins

topography: the natural and human-made features of the Earth's surface

virtual reality: a computer-generated experience that takes place within a simulated environment using headgear or other equipment that shuts out the real world

work-life balance: a term that is used to describe the need to have a healthy balance of time on the job and time spent with family and on leisure activities

Chapter 1

WHAT DO ENTERTAINMENT ENGINEERS DO?

WHAT IS ENGINEERING?

"Engineering combines the fields of science and maths to solve real world problems that improve the world around us," according to the College of Engineering at the University of Maine. There are more than forty engineering specialties—from mechanical and industrial engineering to civil, electronics, and environmental engineering.

Engineers play a role in nearly every area of our lives. When you drive on the highway, take an elevator, or fly on an airplane, you can thank an engineer. When you play video games, use your smartphone, or post on social media, you can thank engineers. And when you drink clean water, get an X-ray, and sit in your warm home as you watch a snowstorm outside, you can thank an engineer. That's just the tip of the iceberg of how you can thank engineers.

Engineers can also be considered inventors, scientists, designers, builders, and visionaries (those who are expert at planning for and predicting future developments). They are troubleshooters and problem-solvers, and some are creative geniuses. There are not many careers where you can take an idea on a piece of paper and turn it into a new pacemaker that saves lives, a system that improves fuel efficiency on cars, or an amusement park with more than fifteen roller coasters.

THE BEST ENGINEERING JOBS

Each year, *U.S. News & World Report* creates a list of the best jobs in the United States. Those that rank high on its list offer an excellent salary, strong employment prospects, many jobs, good **work-life balance**, and low or manageable stress levels. Here were its top engineering-related jobs:

1. Mechanical engineer
2. Civil engineer
3. Cartographer
4. Petroleum engineer
5. Architect
6. Biomedical engineer
7. Environmental engineering technician
8. Environmental engineer

Photo by Bob Hughes

University of Kentucky | see blue.

An entertainment engineer who earned an engineering degree from the University of Kentucky discusses his career

WHAT IS ENTERTAINMENT ENGINEERING?

Every time you ride a roller coaster, visit a waterpark, or attend a mind-blowing theatrical show, you can thank entertainment engineers. These engineers have a unique combination of engineering know-how and art and design skills. Entertainment engineers are both practical and creative. They design, build, troubleshoot, and repair roller coasters; water park rides; interactive exhibits at museums and aquariums; stage components for musical acts, theater performances, and sporting events (such as Super Bowl halftime shows); audio and lighting systems; and many other types of structures and systems that are used to entertain people.

Some people classify entertainment engineers as those who create structures and systems for live entertainment, while others believe that the field of entertainment engineering also includes engineers who perform these tasks for films, television shows, non-live museum exhibitions, and in other settings. This book covers entertainment engineers who work in both areas.

Entertainment engineers typically have degrees in a wide variety of engineering and science disciplines. They often have degrees and training in computer science; civil, structural, industrial, mechanical, electrical, and computer engineering; robotics; acoustics (sound), and other areas. They also have experience and education in art, design, and other creative fields.

Depending on the size of their employer and their job title, entertainment engineers may focus on design, project management, research and development (creating new systems or processes), quality control (making sure everything is built correctly), field service (maintaining and repairing existing

Entertainment engineers have backgrounds in many engineering fields, including industrial engineering.

structures and systems), and sales and customer development. At a small two- or three-person firm, an engineer may do all these tasks and others.

When starting a project, entertainment engineers first meet with the client to discuss its goals and needs. Let's use an example of an amusement park company that hires an entertainment engineering firm to design and oversee the construction of a new roller coaster. The entertainment engineer, designer, architect, and others at the engineering firm meet with company representatives and ask these and many other questions:

- Can you give us a "big picture" description of your project?
- Where will it be built?
- How tall will it be?
- How fast do you want it to go?
- How many park guests will the coaster hold on each ride?

- What is your time frame for completion?
- What type of **multimedia**, **virtual reality**, or other special features would you like the roller coaster to have?

These questions are just the beginning of weeks, and even months, of discussions that will occur between the engineering firm and the client to finalize all aspects of the project. Engineers, architects, and others at the engineering firm also visit the proposed building site to gather information about meteorological conditions (a site with consistently high winds is not the best place for a towering roller coaster), the site's **topography** and soil (some soil types are better at supporting large structures than others), and many other issues.

Entertainment engineers design, build, troubleshoot, and repair all types of rides at amusement parks.

Virtual reality is increasingly being introduced into entertainment settings. Virtual reality technology is used to create the experience of a floating boat.

Entertainment engineers use computer-aided design (CAD) software to create one or more design prototypes. Once the design is approved, work begins on the physical structure. The engineer works closely with architects, surveyors, hydrologists (water experts), engineering technicians, other engineers, construction workers (including construction managers, ironworkers, and electricians), local government officials, and, of course, the client, to build the roller coaster (or other project) to design specifications.

DAY IN THE LIFE: ROLLER COASTER ENGINEER

I've worked as a roller coaster engineer for ten years. I started working as entertainment engineer after five years of employment at a civil engineering firm. My company designs and oversees the construction of roller coasters and other entertainment rides around the world.

I've loved roller coasters since I was a kid. When I was five or six, I remember going to a Six Flags theme park and watching the roller coasters zip around the park, people screaming in joy (or terror?), their arms flailing, and I wanted to see what all the excitement was about. Of course, I wasn't tall enough to ride yet. The first summer that I hit the minimum height requirement, I bugged my parents to take me back to Six Flags. My first ride was on the Demon, a multi-looping roller coaster. At the time, it wasn't the newest or fastest roller coaster, but it was still amazing! After that, I was hooked. I maintain a "bucket list" of roller coasters that I plan to keep checking off till the day I die.

A typical day on the job involves both office and field work. I spend about half my time writing design proposals and coming up with new layouts and design concepts. I'm inspired by past roller coasters, pop culture, and even nature. If I see something cool out in the world, I often say to myself: "I want to put that into the design of the coaster." The rest of the time, I'm out in the field. I travel frequently and meet with clients around the world to try to convince them to buy our roller coasters. My company is currently focusing on developing a strong customer base in South America, so I've recently been to Chile, Uruguay, Paraguay, Argentina, and Panama. I love traveling and seeing new places, but I can see where this might get tiring if you had a family.

Once a client hires us, I work with our construction team as we build the coaster. Although I'm not building the coaster daily, I certainly get my hands dirty when troubleshooting or otherwise pitching in as needed. When the coaster is finished, we ride it as much as necessary (usually fifteen to twenty times) to ensure that it's been built correctly and meets design, safety, and other specifications. We'll often test the coaster in the middle of the night when the park is deserted. It's pretty cool to ride a coaster at night and see the lights of the city, the mountains, or other cool sites.

Many young people ask me if they should become entertainment engineers, and I wholeheartedly tell them, "Yes!" It's a tough field to break into, but well worth the hard work and training.

A roller coaster engineer explains why he loves his career

EXAMPLES OF ENTERTAINMENT ENGINEERING

To get a better understanding of the work of entertainment engineers, let's take a look at some entertainments projects that were recently completed by engineering firms.

DESIGNING AND ENGINEERING A WATER PARK IN A DESERT NATION

The design and engineering firm Atkins provided architecture theming and design; mechanical, electrical, plumbing, and structural engineering expertise; and other services in its role as lead designer of the Yas Waterworld in Abu Dhabi, the capital of the United Arab Emirates. In addition to developing the actual water park, Atkins coordinated work on the park's acoustics, security, and information technology systems.

Yas Waterworld
in Abu Dhabi.

This was a challenging project. Engineers had to design and develop a complex network of underground mechanical, electrical, and plumbing systems, including more than 43.5 miles (70 kilometers) of pipework and cabling. The project was a big success. Yas Waterworld was named one of the world's most sustainable water parks, and it has consistently ranked as one of the top twenty waterparks in the world.

COOL VACATION IDEA

Yas Waterworld in Abu Dhabi features Bandit Bomber, the world's first interactive water and laser roller coaster, as well as Liwa Loop, the region's first looping waterslide. Five of its rides are found nowhere else in the world.

DESIGNING AND BUILDING A STAGE AND MORE FOR A MUSIC STAR

All Access Staging Productions—an entertainment engineering firm with offices in New York, Los Angeles, and London—was hired to create a concert stage for Romeo Santos, a well-known American singer and songwriter. All Access had to create a new design for the stage's support structure because the singer wanted to incorporate a large number of special effects into his concert—including six large moving lighting grid walls. Creating a large stage and a huge lighting system was a challenge.

The solution: design and engineer the large main stage so that it could be divided into six pieces that could be built independently at the venue space and then be quickly put together while the lighting system was also being constructed. All Access' hard work paid off, and the stage and lighting system were ready for Santos's **sound check**.

DESIGNING AND BUILDING THE BATTERY PARK SEAGLASS CAROUSEL

McLaren Engineering Group created a whimsical merry-go-round in New York City's Battery Park that incorporated cutting-edge design, modern multi-axis ride technology, and state-of-the-art multimedia projections, music, and lighting. According to McLaren's website, its Entertainment Division "went the extra mile–delivering complete structural, mechanical, and electrical engineering for the ride system, while also providing the site/civil work for the building. McLaren produced comprehensive 3-D models, performed motion and velocity studies to ensure rider safety, and coordinated on space, geometry, and functional issues to ensure an integrated custom design."

The SeaGlass Carousel in New York City's Battery Park.

DID YOU KNOW?

The oldest roller coaster in operation is Leap-the-Dips at Lakemont Park in Altoona, Pennsylvania, in the United States. It was built in 1902. You can learn more about Leap-the-Dips at www.lakemontparkfun.com.

These are the four oldest roller coasters in the world, according to Coasterpedia.net:

- Leap-the-Dips (1902) at Lakemont Park in the United States
- Scenic Railway (1912) at Luna Park in Australia
- Rutschebanen (1914) at Tivoli Gardens in Denmark
- Wild One (1917) at Six Flags America in the United States

DESIGNING A LAUNCH SIMULATOR AT THE KENNEDY SPACE CENTER

The design and engineering firm BRPH was hired by the Kennedy Space Center in Cape Canaveral, Florida, to create a launch simulator that would allow visitors to experience the sights, sounds, and sensations of a space shuttle launch. According to the BRPH website, "this experience has 'the real stuff.' Designed with input from astronauts who have actually flown on the shuttle, the simulated launch experience allows visitors a once-in-a-lifetime opportunity to ride the space shuttle into orbit. For…five minutes, the pod's forty-four passengers see, feel, and live the trip to 17,500 mph (28,163.5 kph). As the shuttle bay doors open, what follows is a breathtaking view of Earth seldom seen in the first person."

DESIGNING AND BUILDING BATMAN: THE RIDE

ITEC Entertainment was hired by Six Flags Theme Parks to design and build Batman: The Ride for its St. Louis, Missouri, theme park. ITEC describes the ride on its website: "Suspended from the track above in ski lift-style chairs, riders fly at intense speeds countless times over the outside of hairpin turns, vertical loops, a corkscrew, and a one-of-a-kind zero-gravity heartline spin with nothing but air beneath their dangling feet."

MAKING A REPLICA SHIP LOOK REAL FOR A MOVIE

Hopper Engineering Associates created mechanical and electrical systems and structures that realistically simulated the appearance and motion under sail of the *HMS Rose* for the movie *Master and Commander: The Far Side of the World*. The movie was nominated for an Oscar in the "Best Visual Effects" category.

AMAZING ACHIEVEMENTS IN ENGINEERING

The National Academy of Engineering selected the greatest engineering achievements of the twentieth century. Here are the top ten achievements. Visit www.greatachievements.org for the complete list

1. Electrification
2. Automobile
3. Airplane
4. Water Supply and Distribution
5. Electronics
6. Radio and Television
7. Agricultural Mechanization
8. Computers
9. Telephone
10. Air Conditioning and Refrigeration

A theme park engineer at Walt Disney discusses her career and the key traits and educational preparation needed for engineers in this speciality

WORK ENVIRONMENT

Entertainment engineers have a variety of work environments. When assigned to a new project—such as the design, construction, and development of a new amusement park—they visit the site and consult with architects, construction managers, surveyors, and other professionals. The site may be just a muddy field or an abandoned factory. Engineers work outside in all types of weather—from hot, sunny days to rainy or snowy ones. Entertainment engineers also spend a lot of time indoors in their offices or at the offices of clients, developing and discussing design plans. These settings are comfortable and climate-controlled.

Some entertainment engineers travel frequently. In the course of a month, an engineer who is employed by an international engineering consulting firm may have to travel from their home base in Los Angeles to Tokyo, Japan; Shanghai;

Entertainment engineers work outside in all types of weather.

China; and Sydney, Australia, to meet with clients and manage ongoing projects. Some engineers enjoy the opportunity to travel and see the world, while others—often those with families—quickly tire of the constant travel.

Entertainment engineers typically work regular office hours (9 a.m. to 5 p.m.), but they may have to work at night and on weekends when on deadline, or for other reasons.

The workplace atmosphere at an entertainment engineering firm is usually fast-paced and demanding. But many engineers enjoy the busy pace and the opportunity to use their creativity and engineering skills to design the next world-famous roller coaster, water park, or virtual reality flight simulator.

OTHER CAREER OPTIONS IN THE ENTERTAINMENT CONSTRUCTION INDUSTRY

Surveyors use a variety of measuring equipment and technologies to determine property boundaries.

Architects use CAD and drafting and building information modeling software to create designs for houses, theme parks, water parks, factories, and other structures.

Construction managers oversee every aspect of a construction project—from the various types of trades workers (electricians, plumbers, steelworkers, etc.) that do the actual work to managing budgets, ordering supplies and equipment, and ensuring that the job site is safe for workers.

Construction inspectors examine entire buildings, roads, bridges, dams, sewer and water systems, and other structures (including theme parks and other entertainment facilities). Sometimes the structure is being built, or repaired. They also inspect the individual systems—electrical, plumbing, heating/cooling, etc.—that exist in some of these structures.

ADVANCEMENT POSSIBILITIES

Entertainment engineers with advanced education and experience can become *project managers*, who supervise teams of engineers, architects, designers, and technicians. The next level at some firms may be *managing engineer*, who oversees a number of project engineers and their teams. Very large design and engineering firms may employ *chief engineers* or *directors of engineering*, who are responsible for every aspect of engineering at the firm and also have a say in "big picture" decisions regarding company finances, project development, etc. Some engineers decide to launch their own entertainment design firms. Others choose to teach mechanical, civil, or other types of engineering at colleges and universities.

TEXT-DEPENDENT QUESTIONS:

1. What is engineering?
2. What is entertainment engineering?
3. Can you provide an example of a typical entertainment engineering project?

RESEARCH PROJECT:

Interview entertainment engineers in at least three specialties (such as roller coaster design, water park design, and interactive exhibits). Write a report that compares and contrasts the job duties in each specialty. Present it to your class. Which career path do you think best fits your skills and interests? Spend some additional time exploring this field.

Chapter 2

TERMS OF
THE TRADE

3-D printer: Technology that manufactures three-dimensional solid objects from a digital file. It can make anything from tools and toys to metal machine parts and building components.

3-D project mapping: A process in which several projection sources are used to project a three-dimensional image on an object, typically on a building or cliff face. The images constantly spin, shift, and change color to create a stunning animation-like effect.

acceleration: When something moves faster or something happens more quickly.

acoustics: A branch of physics that focuses on the study and properties of sound.

aerodynamics: The interaction between the atmosphere and moving objects.

alternating current (AC): An electric charge that changes direction periodically; it is used to deliver power to houses and office buildings.

animatronics: The process of using motors and/or cable-pulled devices to make an inanimate object move and act like a human, animal, or other moving object.

artificial intelligence: The simulation of human intelligence by machinery and computer systems.

attraction and control monitoring system: A system that is used to monitor and direct the overall experience at an attraction (water park, virtual reality exhibit, etc.). It is used to interface with animation, audio, video, lighting, and special effects features.

augmented reality: A computer-generated system that combines a virtual environment with imaginary elements that are introduced to a real environment; examples include Snapchat lenses and the game Pokémon Go.

blueprint: A reproduction of a technical plan for the construction of a home or other structure. Blueprints are created by licensed architects.

budget: A financial plan that details the amount of money that is available to spend on a project and its various components.

building codes: A series of rules established by local, state, regional, and national governments that ensure safe construction.

building information modeling software: A computer application that uses a 3-D model–based process that helps construction, architecture, and engineering professionals to more efficiently plan, design, build, and manage buildings and infrastructure.

building materials: Natural and human-made materials such as wood, concrete, steel, and asphalt that are used to construct and build things.

centripetal force: The force that keeps a person or object on a curved path when the object that they are on (such as a merry-go-round or roller coaster) is moving.

civil engineering: The use of scientific and engineering principles to design and build roads, dams, bridges, amusement parks, water supply and sewage treatment systems, buildings, airports, tunnels, and other infrastructure projects and systems.

combustion: A chemical process in which fuel reacts rapidly with oxygen and gives off heat.

composite material: A substance made of two or more materials that, when combined, has different chemical or physical properties from the original substances.

computer-aided design (CAD): The process of using software to create architectural plans, blueprints, or artwork.

consultant: An experienced professional who is self-employed and provides expertise about a particular subject.

cost estimate: A data-based analysis of how much materials, equipment, and labor will cost to complete a project.

direct current (DC): An electric charge that only travels in one direction; devices that plug into the wall with an alternating current (AC) adapter are powered by a battery, or they use a USB cable for power that relies on direct current.

drones: Unmanned aerial vehicles that are made of lightweight composite materials that reduce weight and increase maneuverability. In the

entertainment industry they are used to gather information about construction sites; to create beautiful, multimedia shows; and for other purposes.

electrical engineering: The use of scientific and engineering principles to develop and build electrical systems such as electric motors, radar and navigation systems, and power generation equipment.

electronics engineering: The use of scientific and engineering principles to develop and build electronic equipment, such as broadcast and communications systems.

energy: Thermal (heat), light (radiant), kinetic (motion), electrical, chemical, nuclear, or gravitational energy that is harnessed to perform the functions of life.

engineering: The use of science and engineering principles to design, build, test, troubleshoot, and repair products, systems, structures, and infrastructure (highways, dams, etc.).

environmental engineering: The use of scientific and engineering principles to solve environmental issues (pollution, noise, damage to rare or endangered species, etc.) at an existing or potential construction site.

feasibility study: A fact-based investigation of the expected financial potential (profits) of a project and its expected construction and operating costs.

finite element analysis (FEA): The use of computers and mathematical equations to solve engineering questions relating to structural analysis, heat transfer, fluid flow, and other areas by breaking down the issue into smaller, simpler parts that are called "finite elements." The use of FEA techniques reduces the number of physical prototypes needed and helps design engineers improve productivity.

fluid power: A form of power transmission that uses hydraulic or pneumatic technologies to transmit power from one location to another.

force: Any type of push or pull.

friction: The force that slows two objects down because they are interacting with one another.

gravitational force: The amount of force exerted on an object by the Earth's gravity at sea level; it is commonly referred to as **g-force**.

gravity: The force by which a planet or other celestial (space) body draws objects toward its center.

green construction: The process of planning, designing, building, and operating structures in an environmentally responsible manner.

hardware engineering: The use of scientific and engineering principles to research, design, develop, and test networks, routers, processors, circuit boards, memory devices, and other types of technology.

health and safety engineering: The use of scientific and engineering principles to develop procedures and design systems to protect people from injury or illness and property from damage.

hydraulic technologies: Those that use liquid fluid (liquid or gas) power to perform a task.

industrial engineering: The use of scientific and engineering principles to identify and eliminate wasted energy, building materials, work hours, etc., in manufacturing and construction processes. Industrial engineers study ways to improve worker productivity, reduce energy and material use, and improve the performance of machinery.

inertia: The concept that an object at rest is apt to stay at rest and that an object that is in motion is apt to stay in motion.

infrastructure: In relation to the construction industry, the systems of a city, region, or nation such as communication, sewage, water, transportation, bridges, dams, and electric.

inversion: The part of a roller coaster that turns riders upside down; it is also known as a **loop**, **hoop**, or **loop de loops** (when at least two inversions are present).

kinetic (working) energy: Energy that is in motion. There are five types of kinetic energy: thermal, radiant, motion, electrical, and auditory.

load: The amount of weight that is distributed throughout a structure.

mechanical engineering: A broad engineering discipline that uses scientific and engineering principles to design and oversee the manufacture of a wide variety of products and systems, including electric generators, refrigeration and air-conditioning systems, elevators and escalators, amusement park rides, internal combustion engines, and steam and gas turbines.

pile: A long, round pole that is made from steel, wood, or concrete and is driven into the soil by a pile driver (a noisy machine).

potential (stored) energy: Energy that can be stored and used when needed. There are four types of potential energy: chemical, elastic, nuclear, and gravitational.

pneumatic technologies: Those that use a gas (usually compressed air) to perform a task.

pressure: Force that is applied or distributed over a particular area.

pyrotechnics: A fireworks display.

reinforced concrete: Concrete in which steel bars or mesh has been added to increase its strength in tension.

retrofit: To add a component or system to a building or other structure that it did not have when it was constructed.

robotics: An interdisciplinary area of science and mechanical, electronic engineering, computer, and other types of engineering that is used to create

technology (robots) and their operating systems that are used to perform tasks more efficiently and less expensively than can be done by humans.

schematic diagram: An illustration of the components of a system—or, in the instance of entertainment engineering, an entire theme park or water park—that uses abstract, graphic symbols instead of realistic pictures or illustrations.

software: A program that operates a computer or allows a user to perform a specific task.

software engineering: The use of scientific and engineering principles to design software applications, software that operates computer and other systems, and other types of software.

special effects: Artificial visual or mechanical effects that create imaginary realities in movies, television shows, amusement parks, theatrical productions, museum exhibits, and in other settings. Mechanical effects are created by explosives, makeup, prosthetics, wires, puppets, and miniature models. Computer animation and computer-generated imagery are also used to create special effects.

steel: An alloy of carbon and iron that is strong and hard, and that can be easily bent or shaped without breaking or cracking.

structural engineering: A subfield of civil engineering that involves the design, construction, testing, troubleshooting, and repair of buildings, bridges, amusement park rides, and other structures.

structure: Something that is constructed or built, such as a building, dam, amusement park ride, or theatrical stage.

sustainability: In the construction industry, an emphasis on building practices that save energy or reduce energy output.

tension: A stretching force that pulls a material.

thermodynamics: A branch of physics that deals with the energy and work of a system.

torsion: An action that twists a material.

transfer of energy: The process of converting one form of energy (such as the potential energy when a roller coaster climbs higher on a hill to start its run) to another form (such as kinetic, the energy of motion once the coaster goes down the hill).

valleying: A serious situation that occurs when a roller coaster loses momentum and is unable to make it to the next "hill" or inversion.

velocity: The combination of the speed and the direction in which an object is traveling.

virtual reality: A computer-generated experience that takes place within a simulated environment using headgear or other equipment that shuts out the real world.

WORDS TO UNDERSTAND

ABET: a nonprofit, non-governmental organization that accredits college and university programs in engineering, engineering technology, applied and natural science, and computing in the United States and around the world

accreditation: the process of being evaluated by a governing body (such as ABET) and being approved as providing quality coursework, products, or services

associate's degree: a degree that requires a two-year course of study after high school

master's degree: a two-year, graduate-level degree that is earned after a student first completes a four-year bachelor's degree

Chapter 3

PREPARING FOR THE FIELD AND MAKING A LIVING

EDUCATIONAL PATHS

If you want to become an entertainment engineer, you'll first need to earn at least a bachelor's degree (an education credential that requires a four-year course of study after high school) in general engineering or a specialty degree such as software, electrical, or mechanical engineering. In some countries, aspiring engineers prepare for the field by participating in apprenticeships. You can also receive engineering training in the military, but you may still need to earn a degree or complete an apprenticeship once you are discharged (released) from the military.

Regardless of how you train to become an engineer, you'll also need to take specialized entertainment engineering classes that are offered by associations and colleges to help develop specialized skills and knowledge. Many students participate in an internship at an entertainment engineering company to build their skills. An internship is a paid or unpaid learning opportunity in which a student works at a business to get experience; it can last anywhere from a few weeks to a year. The following sections provide more information on educational preparation.

HIGH SCHOOL CLASSES

Many high school classes will help you to prepare for work in entertainment engineering. Here are some suggestions:

- shop
- engineering
- mathematics (algebra, trigonometry, calculus)
- physics

Aspiring entertainment engineers should take as many computer science classes as possible.

- chemistry
- Earth science
- meteorology
- computer science
- computer-aided design
- art and design
- social studies
- English and speech
- foreign languages (these will come in handy if you work outside your home country)
- business, marketing, and accounting (if you plan to start your own company)

Learn how students at Purdue University use virtual reality to design roller coasters

COLLEGES AND UNIVERSITIES

Many engineers train for the field by earning at least a bachelor's degree in general engineering or a specialty such as electrical, mechanical, industrial, or computer engineering. If you want to become a manager and/or get the best-paying jobs, you'll need to earn a **master's degree** in engineering or an engineering specialty. College students typically complete at least one internship as part of their training.

The University of Nevada at Las Vegas (www.unlv.edu/eed) is the only college or university in the United States to offer a degree in entertainment engineering and design. Its multidisciplinary program (education from many fields) combines technical theater and engineering to prepare students for careers in the entertainment industry. Typical classes in this program include:

- Materials Science and Fabrication Techniques

- Basic Kinetic Structures

- Multi-Media Design

- Computer-Aided Design

- Design for Live Entertainment

- Programmable Systems for the Entertainment Industry

- Design Communications

- Construction Materials and Methods

- Automation

- Robotics

- Structural Design and Rigging

- Entertainment Venue Design

Engineers frequently use computer-aided design software in their work, so it's a good idea to take CAD classes in school.

- Acoustics
- Various Engineering Classes

Some colleges and universities offer degrees in entertainment design and technology. These programs are less focused on engineering but could provide preparation for jobs that are more design-oriented. One example is Valencia College in Orlando, Florida, which offers an **associate's degree** in entertainment design and technology. Students can specialize in audiovisual event production, live show production, and production design. You can learn more about this program by visiting https://net1.valenciacollege.edu/future-students/degree-options/associates/entertainment-design-and-technology. Eastern Michigan University (Ypsilanti) offers a bachelor of arts in entertainment design and technology. More information on this program is available at https://catalog.emich.edu.

Some students train for a career in engineering by participating in an apprenticeship.

Some aspiring engineers prepare for the field by earning an associate's degree in engineering or engineering technology, then transfer to a four-year college to earn a bachelor's degree in an engineering specialty.

APPRENTICESHIPS

Although this approach is not as popular as earning a degree, some engineers train for the field by completing an apprenticeship program. In the United States, apprenticeship programs typically last three to five years, although some programs are shorter. During each year in the program, trainees complete 2,000 hours of on-the-job training and 144 hours of related classroom instruction. Entry requirements vary by program, but typical requirements include:

- minimum age of eighteen (in Canada and some other countries, the minimum age is sixteen)

- high school education

- one year of high school algebra

- qualifying score on an aptitude test

- drug free (illegal drugs)

There are pros and cons to participating in an engineering apprenticeship. Unlike in college—where students have to pay tuition (money to attend school)—apprentices do not have to pay tuition, and they receive a salary that increases as they gain experience. Training may, but not always, be shorter than the four-year requirement for a bachelor's degree. On the other hand, some employers prefer to hire job candidates who have earned a college degree. In some countries, engineers whose work could affect the life, health, or safety of the public must be registered according to government regulations. In the United States, engineers in this category must receive a degree from a college or university engineering program that has received **accreditation** from **ABET**, have at least four years of experience, pass a written examination, and meet other criteria.

Here are some websites to check out to learn more about apprenticeship opportunities in select countries:

- United States: www.doleta.gov/OA/sainformation.cfm

- Canada: www.canada.ca/en/employment-social-development/services/apprentices.html

- United Kingdom: www.gov.uk/education/apprenticeships-traineeships-and-internships

Enlisting in the military is a good way to learn basic engineering and technical skills that can prepare you for a career in entertainment engineering.

If you live in another country, contact your country's department of labor for more information.

MILITARY

In the military, you won't learn how to build roller coasters, merry-go-rounds, or virtual reality rides, but you will get the chance to develop your engineering chops. All five U.S. military branches (Air Force, Army, Coast Guard, Marines, and Navy), as well as militaries in other countries, offer training in one or more engineering careers. For example, electrical and electronics engineering trainees design, develop, install, test, and repair electrical and electronic devices such as radar, missile guidance systems, and communication equipment. While not every engineering skill you learn in the military can be used in the entertainment industry, many can.

In the U.S. military, training opportunities are also available in aerospace, civil, environmental, industrial safety and health, and industrial engineering. Additionally, the military offers computer-related training that can provide good preparation for some positions in the entertainment industry.

Receiving your training via the military is a good strategy if you don't mind following orders and agree to serve from to two to four years. You also earn a salary during your time in the military. Keep in mind that just because you want to become an engineer, the military doesn't have to make you one (unless it promises to do so in your enlistment contract). The Army, for example, might think you're a better fit as a cook, driver, or infantryman. When talking with a recruiter, be sure to get a clear picture of how long you will have to serve and what type of career you will work in.

MAJOR EMPLOYERS OF ENTERTAINMENT ENGINEERS

- Entertainment design and engineering companies
- Media companies
- Amusement parks
- Waterparks
- Consulting firms

- Theaters
- Film and television production companies
- Convention services firms
- TV stations

Waterparks are just one type of entertainment venue that are designed by entertainment engineers.

GETTING A JOB

It's certainly not time to get a job, but it's never too early to learn how the job search process works. When it comes time to look for your first part- or full-time job, or an internship, you'll be ahead of the game and will have already "hacked" the job search. Here are some common job search methods for job seekers.

USE YOUR NETWORK

"Many individuals have attributed their personal and business success on their ability to network," according to The Institution of Engineering and Technology, one of the world's largest engineering associations. "Networking and the development of good contacts can generate a variety of opportunities."

So, what is a network? A network is simply a group of people whom you connect with to get information, or contact when you otherwise need help with something (homework, a ride to baseball practice, etc.). If you have family, friends, and classmates (which you do, of course), you have a network. This type of network is called your "personal network." As you move into high school, college, and working, you'll also become part of a professional network that includes your teachers, coaches, bosses, internship directors, and people whom you meet online, including at social networking sites such as LinkedIn or MeetUp.com.

You can use your network to:

- talk with people who love building things and exploring science, engineering, and technology (especially as they relate to the entertainment industry)

- talk with your math and science teachers about potential career paths and what it takes to become an engineer

- attend engineering, science, and environmental competitions and events

- start a school or local club that focuses on engineering

- visit websites that offer discussion boards for current or aspiring engineers

Here are some tips to keep in mind as you network:

- Stay in regular touch with your network so that when you need something, your contacts will remember you and be more willing to help.

- Be genuine. Don't just network to collect names, but get to really know people and develop relationships that can sometimes turn into lifelong friendships.

- At first, use email as a low-stress strategy to contact people whom you don't know instead of a phone call.

- Remember that networking is a two-way street: always try to help others in your network if you're asked.

- Keep networking once you get an internship or job. You never know when you'll need help from your network.

DAY IN THE LIFE: ENTERTAINMENT ENGINEER

I've worked as an entertainment engineer for twenty years. Most of my time has been spent providing engineering solutions in the theatrical/concert industry in Las Vegas; New York City; Branson, Missouri; and other places. I really love my job because I like the fact that the work always changes, I get the chance to solve problems and use my creativity, and I get to work in a field (theatrical productions/concerts) that I love.

My firm designs new systems (lighting, audio, multimedia, etc.) and structures (complex stages, etc.), but also spends a lot of time repairing and retrofitting existing systems and structures. Let me tell you about a major project that I worked on recently at a hotel/casino in Las Vegas.

This popular show is being presented by what I'll call a "modern circus company" (I'm not allowed to give client names). The production includes a 130-ton stage that rises from below ground level, tilts 180 degrees, and rotates 360 degrees. The performers act, fly, climb, fight, and do many other actions while the stage is in various positions.

This project was challenging. The maintenance crew was having problems with the stage's hydraulics, motion control, and other systems, and shows were being canceled because of the issues. The problem was that the system that powered and moved the stage was getting old. The stage moved thirty times each performance, which we determined created thirty-five opportunities for malfunction. Also, 16 seconds of lead time was needed to make the stage move each time, and the frequent stops and starts were causing excessive wear and tear on the brakes. This was adding up to expensive maintenance and repair costs.

My firm was brought in to study and provide suggestions to fix these problems. I worked over the course of a year and a half to develop a retrofit and motion system upgrade. Most of our onsite work was conducted during scheduled shutdowns. I won't go into tremendous detail, but after we completed our work, the new system we developed only had one or two single points of potential failure (down from thirty-five). In our new design, the brakes were only used once during each production. Hydraulic pressure controls were used to hold the stage in different positions, as needed, during performances. This saved the theater company a lot of money on brake maintenance. We reduced the 16 seconds of lead time for stage moves to milliseconds through

the use of a closed-loop position control system. The stage movements became smoother, and the number of breakdowns dropped dramatically. No shows have been canceled since we did our work.

I loved working on this project because it was both challenging and rewarding. We took something that was old and malfunctioning and turned it into something that worked nearly flawlessly. The theater company and the actors and other performers loved the new stage. And I loved the first show I got to attend after completing the project! It was fun being part of something big and seeing the results firsthand.

CHECK OUT JOB BOARDS

Many people search for jobs by visiting internet job boards, at which a variety of organizations list open positions. Engineering associations and businesses are just a few of the organizations that offer job boards. At many of these sites, you can search by job type, employer name, salary, geographic area, and other criteria.

While you're not yet ready to look for a full-time job, you should still check out job boards to see what types of skills and education are in demand. If you're in high school, you can use job boards to find an internship or a part-time job. Here are a few popular engineering job boards:

- www.nspe.org/resources/career-center/job-board/
  job-board

- http://jobs.teaconnect.org

- www.waterparks.org/jobboard

- www.engineerjobs.com

- www.engineeringjobs.net

- https://jobs.iaapa.org

These are some general career boards that offer entertainment engineering and general engineering job listings:

- www.indeed.com

- www.linkedin.com

- www.usajobs.gov (U.S. government job board)

- www.jobbank.gc.ca (Canadian government job board)

- www.gov.uk/jobsearch (United Kingdom government job board)

JOIN AND USE THE RESOURCES OF PROFESSIONAL ASSOCIATIONS

Professional engineering associations are great resources for engineering students and engineers. They offer membership (including categories for students), networking events, job listings, training opportunities, and certification. Certification is a credential that you earn by passing a test and meeting other requirements. Certified worked have a better chance of landing a job than those who are not certified. They also often earn higher salaries than those who are not certified.

One good resource is the Themed Entertainment Association (TEA, www.teaconnect.org). This international association represents people who design

Making a lot of money is great, but doing something that you love—such as designing the lighting and sounds systems for a Las Vegas show—is the key to happiness in life.

and build theme parks, water parks, museums, zoos, multimedia spectaculars, resorts, and other entertainment and leisure facilities. The TEA offers job listings, college clubs, and information on education and careers in the themed entertainment industry.

Here are some major professional associations for engineers around the world:

- National Society of Professional Engineers (United States): www.nspe.org

- American Society for Engineering Education: www.asee.org

- The Institution of Engineering and Technology (United Kingdom): www.theiet.org

- Engineers Canada: https://engineerscanada.ca

- Engineers Australia: www.engineersaustralia.org.au

There are also associations that represent engineers in various engineering specialties, such as the American Society of Mechanical Engineers (www.asme. org) and the Institute of Electric and Electronics Engineers (www.ieee.org). If you want to learn about education and careers in an engineering specialty, these organizations are good resources.

SALARIES FOR MECHANICAL ENGINEERS BY U.S. STATE

Many entertainment engineers have degrees in mechanical engineering. Earnings for mechanical engineers vary by state based on demand and other factors. Here are the five states where employers pay the highest average salary and the states in which employers pay the lowest salaries.

Highest Average Salaries:

1. Alaska: $132,100
2. New Mexico: $108,990
3. Texas: $106,020
4. Maryland: $104,250
5. California: $104,030

Lowest Average Salaries:

1. South Dakota: $74,100
2. Iowa: $74,120
3. Arkansas: $74,330
4. North Dakota: $76,060
5. Wisconsin: $78,010

Source: U.S. Department of Labor

HOW MUCH CAN I EARN?

Earnings for entertainment engineers vary by job title, engineering specialty, educational background, the worker's experience level, whether they work full or part time, and other factors. For example, an entertainment engineer with a bachelor's degree will typically earn less money than an engineer who has a master's degree. An engineer with twenty years of experience will make more money than someone who is just hired out of college. Engineers who live in places where the entertainment industry is located—such as Las Vegas or Los Angeles—usually earn more than those who work in areas where there is less demand for these specialized engineers.

Since entertainment engineers have a variety of engineering degrees, it's a good idea to look at the salaries of engineers by specialty. Here are some salary ranges for engineers in various specialties, according to the U.S. Department of Labor:

- Electrical engineers: $60,250 to $150,340+
- Electronics engineers (except computer): $64,030 to $160,360+
- Hardware engineers: $66,290 to $176,900+
- Industrial engineers: $55,230 to $130,930+
- Mechanical engineers: $55,310 to $133,900+

GOOD ADVICE

While it's great that entertainment engineers earn a lot of money, you shouldn't choose a career based on the high salary. You should find a career that excites you and makes you want to go to work every day. If a career in entertainment engineering fit this description, that's great! But if not, many other exciting careers are available.

What's clear is that regardless of their specialty, entertainment engineers earn excellent salaries. In fact, industrial engineers (the lowest paid engineers) earn higher minimum salaries ($55,230) than the average salary ($50,620) for all workers in the United States.

Entertainment engineers who work full-time (35–40 hours a week) often receive fringe benefits such as health insurance, paid vacation and sick days, and other perks. Self-employed workers—those who work for themselves, rather than for an employer—do not receive these benefits.

TEXT-DEPENDENT QUESTIONS:

1. What are some typical college classes for those who want to become entertainment engineers?
2. What are the benefits of joining engineering associations?
3. How much can entertainment engineers earn?

RESEARCH PROJECT:

Learn more about Newton's Laws of Motion at www. physics4kids.com/files/motion_laws.html. Knowledge of these laws is essential for success in engineering. How do these laws apply to the design, construction, and operation of roller coasters?

WORDS TO UNDERSTAND

conference: an event at which members of an organization, and sometimes the public, meet to discuss and learn more about a particular topic, such as engineering or technology

negotiate: to have a discussion in order to reach an agreement to work together on a project or to meet other goals

scholarships: money that is awarded to students to pay for college and other types of education; it does not have to be paid back

teacher-mentor: a teacher who serves as the adult leader of a school group or club

Chapter 4

KEY SKILLS AND METHODS OF EXPLORATION

SKILL BUILDING LEADS TO SUCCESS

It takes a variety of technical and soft skills to be a successful entertainment engineer. Soft skills are personal abilities that people need to develop to be successful on the job. These include a good work ethic, the ability to work as a member of a team, positivity, flexibility, and conflict resolution skills. Below are some key traits for entertainment engineers.

COMMUNICATION AND INTERPERSONAL SKILLS

Engineers need excellent communication and interpersonal skills to be able to effectively work as a member of a team and explain their ideas and findings to clients, who do not typically have an engineering or science background. For

Entertainment engineers need strong interpersonal skills because they frequently work as part of a team to complete projects.

example, engineers might have to use their communication skills to explain why a particular mechanical system is a better fit for the job because it is easier to service, quieter, more energy efficient, and less expensive than a better-known system. Engineers also need strong writing skills because they frequently write project proposals and reports. If your writing is confusing and full of grammatical errors, you won't be employed for long.

PASSION

Many people want to become entertainment engineers, so hiring managers and bosses are always looking for people who are excited about their jobs. Each day, you need to be enthusiastic as you go about your work—whether it's designing and building an amazing roller coaster (your dream job) or preparing a detailed report on structural issues with an existing coaster (a task you dread).

DETAIL-ORIENTED PERSONALITY

An improperly built roller coaster, interactive museum exhibit, or stage can be dangerous—and even deadly. As a result, engineers must be very attentive to detail during every stage of the project—from the blueprint and schematic phase to the construction process to the testing, troubleshooting, and final product launch stages. If you own your own business, you'll need to be organized and detail-oriented in order to keep track of customer appointments, employee payroll (the money you pay to your workers in exchange for their work), invoicing (charging customers for the work that you do), and other important office responsibilities.

TROUBLESHOOTING ABILITY AND PATIENCE

You must be able to think on your feet as you test and troubleshoot systems or try to repair a malfunctioning roller coaster. For example, if a coaster gets stuck, you'll need to determine if the problem is caused by a faulty sensor, an electrical malfunction, or another issue. You also need to be patient and calm under pressure, because your first (or second, or third) solution for an issue may not work.

TECHNICAL, SCIENTIFIC, AND COMPUTER SKILLS

Successful engineers are knowledgeable about physics, Earth science, geology, meteorology, and other scientific and technical areas. They also must be knowledgeable about construction practices and materials—specifically those related to entertainment systems and structures. Finally, familiarity with software and computer systems is important because engineers use technology every day. They use CAD programs such as Vectorworks, AutoCAD, Inventor, and SketchUp to create blueprints, schematics, and other designs; databases to record and analyze information about a project; and project management software to manage complex products and communicate with and manage team members who may be working all over the world.

BUSINESS SKILLS

If you own an engineering firm, you won't just be an engineer anymore. Business owners must be marvelous marketers, sales whizzes, and social media experts.

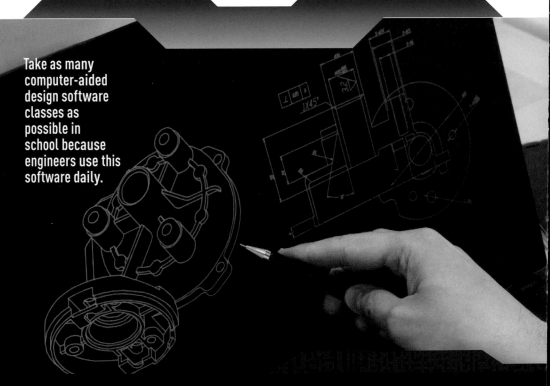

Take as many computer-aided design software classes as possible in school because engineers use this software daily.

You'll also need to learn how to bid on jobs, perform basic accounting tasks, manage staff, and do whatever else it takes to make your business a success.

OTHER IMPORTANT TRAITS

Engineers need many other traits to be successful on the job. Here are a few more to develop:

- Time-management
- Creativity
- Team player
- Curiosity
- Willingness to continue to learn throughout your career

EXPLORING ENGINEERING AS A STUDENT

There are many ways to learn more about engineering and careers in the field. Here are some popular methods of exploration.

JOIN THE TECHNOLOGY STUDENT ASSOCIATION (TSA)

If you're a middle school or high school student and interested in science, technology, engineering, and mathematics, consider joining TSA (www. tsaweb.org). It's the oldest student membership organization dedicated exclusively to students who are enrolled in engineering and technology education classes in middle and high schools. TSA offers sixty competitions at its annual **conference**—including those in animatronics, CAD, engineering, electrical applications, engineering design, mechanical engineering, microcontroller design, scientific visualization, structural design and engineering, system control technology, and technology problem-solving.

The TSA also provides opportunities to develop your leadership skills, perform community service, and compete for money for college. Ask your science teacher or school counselor if your school has a TSA chapter and, if not, ask them to start one.

START A SCIENCE OR ENGINEERING CLUB

Your middle school or high school may already have such a club. If so, that's great. Such clubs are an excellent way to learn more about engineering and science, how to use tools, and what your potential career paths are. If your school doesn't have a club, start one! Your science teacher can help you get organized.

In an engineering club, you'll get the chance to interact with people just like you who like to design and build things. Your club can tackle fun projects such as building a roller coaster or Ferris wheel model using art supplies and items you can find around your house. Your group can also visit the offices of an entertainment engineering firm, or even visit a construction site where an amusement park or water park is being built. Finally, your **teacher-mentor** might be able to set up a presentation by an entertainment engineer. Try to learn as much as you can about engineering in middle and high school. That way, you'll be better prepared when it comes time to go to college.

LEARN HOW TO BUILD A MINI ROLLER COASTER

You don't have to wait till you get to college to get hands-on experience in entertainment engineering. There are many fun projects you can try to learn what it's like to be an entertainment engineer. One involves building a mini roller coaster by using materials you have at home or buy at a hardware store. Follow the instructions at the Museum of Science and Industry Chicago's website, www.msichicago.org/experiment/hands-on-science/roller-coaster (or check out videos on YouTube.com) to build the roller coaster. Get your friends involved. Try to include at least one loop, hill, and jump in your design.

As you build your coaster, ask yourself the following questions to learn more about the challenges that engineers face:

- How does the height of the hills affect the speed of the coaster?

- Should all the hills be the same height? Why or why not?

- How does the placement of loops affect the speed performance of the coaster?

- Did you add any design elements that caused your coaster to crash or get stuck? If so, how did you fix these issues?

- What would you do to make your coaster go faster? Slower?

ATTEND AN ENGINEERING SUMMER CAMP

Summer camps and workshops are offered by colleges, high schools, community groups, museums, companies, and other organizations that want to help young people learn more about engineering, science, mathematics, and other fields. One such opportunity is available from the National Student Leadership Conference. It offers a nine-day summer engineering program for high school students (www.nslcleaders.org/youth-leadership-programs/engineering-summer-programs). The program is held two to four times each summer in six U.S. cities. If you participate in this program, you'll learn about civil, electrical, mechanical, and other engineering specialties. And you'll get a chance to talk with a variety of engineering professionals who will help you learn more about careers in engineering.

Ask your high school counselor or science teacher to help you find engineering camps in your area. You can also check out the websites of local colleges and engineering associations to find opportunities.

A FEW THINGS TO REMEMBER ABOUT CAMPS

Some are free, while others require a fee to attend. Some camps offer **scholarships** to campers. Residential camps are where you stay overnight and at day camps, you go home after each session. But don't worry—most residential camps don't involve tents and bug spray! Instead you'll stay in college dormitories or other comfortable buildings. And keep in mind that many camps only have a small number of spots available, so be sure to apply early.

Here are a few examples of well-known camps in the United States. Camps are also available in other countries.

Watch a group of high school students participate in the Marshmallow Challenge, a competition that helps them to develop their design and engineering skills

- Massachusetts Institute of Technology: https://mitadmissions.org/apply/prepare/summer

- University of Arizona: www.engineering.arizona.edu/k12/ k12_SEA

- University of Wisconsin-Madison: www.engr.wisc.edu/ academics/student-services/diversity-programs/engineering-summer-program

FINDING MORE PROGRAMS

Many other colleges, organizations, and businesses offer engineering, science, and mathematics camps. Contact schools and organizations in your area to learn more and visit the following websites.

- www.engineeringedu.com/camps.php
- www.teenlife.com/category/summer/engineering-summer-programs
- http://careercornerstone.org/pcprogproj.htm

PARTICIPATE IN A COMPETITION

Engineering contests are an excellent way to build your skills and make new friends. Competitions are offered by regional, national, or international associations; corporations; schools; and other organizations. Check out the following competitions:

TEAMS (TESTS OF ENGINEERING APTITUDE, MATHEMATICS AND SCIENCE)

This one-day competition for middle and high school students consists of teams of four to eight students working together. They have to answer multiple-choice questions, complete an essay, and finish a design/build challenge that's based on themes highlighted by the National Academy of Engineering Grand Challenges. Learn more at www.tsaweb.org/competitions-programs/teams.

SKILLS COMPÉTENCES CANADA

This nonprofit organization seeks to encourage Canadian youth to pursue careers in the skilled trades and technology sectors. Its National Competition allows young people to participate in more than forty skilled trade and technology competitions, including Mechanical Engineering, Computer-Aided Design, Robotics, Electronics, and Architectural Technology and Design. Visit http://skillscompetencescanada.com/en/skills-canada-national-competition to learn more about this program.

SkillsUSA

SkillsUSA is a national membership organization for middle school, high school, and college students who are preparing for careers in technical, trade, and skilled service occupations. Some of the competitions that will be of interest to aspiring engineers include Electronics Technology, Engineering Technology/ Design, Mechatronics, Related Technical Math, Principles of Engineering/ Technology, and Robotics and Automation Technology. SkillsUSA works directly with high schools and colleges, so ask your school counselor or teacher if it is an option for you. Learn more at www.skillsusa.org.

One way to learn more about engineering is to participate in robotics competitions.

Students participate in a contest that required them to build and race autonomous vehicles.

OTHER COMPETITIONS

For more competitions, visit

- www.engineergirl.org/250/Contests
- http://careercornerstone.org/pcprogproj.htm.

OTHER WAYS TO LEARN MORE ABOUT ENGINEERING AND SCIENCE

- Take classes in science, engineering, robotics, computer science, and related fields in high school

- Participate in science fairs

- Get a summer job at an amusement park or theater

- Read books and watch videos about the entertainment industry and engineering

- Visit the websites of college and university engineering programs

- Talk to your school counselor about career opportunities in engineering

Learning about robotics during science class is a good way to build your entertainment engineering skills.

JOIN THE SCOUTS

The Girl Scouts and Boy Scouts are membership organizations for girls and boys ages roughly five to eighteen (age ranges vary by country and group). These organizations help you to be a better person and teach you all kinds of things that you didn't know before. When you learn something new in scouts, you usually receive a merit badge or other type of award.

The Boy Scouts of America (www.scouting.org) is open to both boys and girls. Scouts can earn a merit badge in Engineering by providing an oral report on a type of product that was created by engineers, by talking with engineers about their careers, and by fulfilling other requirements. If you're a girl, members of the Girl Scouts of the United States of America (www.girlscouts.org) can earn Mechanical Engineering, Robotics, and Science and Technology merit badges.

Scouting is not just for those who live in the United States. In fact, the Boy Scouts were founded in Great Britain more than 100 years ago. Scouting organizations in Great Britain include The Scout Association (https://scouts.org.uk) and British Boy Scouts and British Girl Scouts Association (https://bbsandbgs.org.uk). If you live in Canada, you can join Scouts Canada (www.scouts.ca).

JOB SHADOW AN ENGINEER

It's one thing to read about careers, but it's even better to see firsthand what's involved in a particular job. You can do this by participating in a job shadowing experience, which involves observing workers as they do their jobs. For example, you could watch an entertainment engineer in her design studio as she creates the blueprints and schematic designs for a 100,000 square foot (9,290.3 square meters) luxury waterpark that features five slides, a rapid river, three levels, and tubing rides that are accentuated with LED light displays and music. Or you could follow an entertainment engineer as he visits an amusement park that is under construction, or watch engineers who specialize in sales **negotiate** a deal in the boardroom of an entertainment company such as Disney or Six Flags.

Ask your school counselor or science teacher to help arrange a job shadowing experience with an entertainment engineer. Youth organizations, such as Junior Achievement, also offer job shadowing experiences. You should also consider contacting local mechanical, civil, or electrical engineering associations to see if they can help set up a job shadowing experience.

A student (left) job shadows two engineers.

SOURCES OF ADDITIONAL EXPLORATION

Contact the following organizations for more information on education and careers in engineering, certification, and membership:

American Academy of Environmental Engineers and Scientists
www.aaees.org

American Society for Engineering Education
www.asee.org

American Society of Civil Engineers (international)
www.asce.org

American Society of Mechanical Engineers International
www.asme.org

Institute of Electrical and Electronics Engineers (international)
www.ieee.org

Institute of Industrial and Systems Engineers
www.iise.org

Institution of Civil Engineers (United Kingdom)
www.ice.org.uk/about-ice

International Association of Amusement Parks and Attractions
www.iaapa.org

National Society of Professional Engineers (United States)
www.nspe.org/resources/students

World Waterpark Association
www.waterparks.org

PARTICIPATE IN AN INFORMATION INTERVIEW

An information interview involves asking an entertainment engineer questions to learn more about their career. You can do this in person or via email, Skype, or a phone conversation. Here are some questions to ask during the interview:

- Can you tell me about a day in your life on the job?

- Do you have to travel for your job? If so, where have you traveled?

- What are the most important personal and professional qualities for people in your career?

- What do you like best and least about your job?

- What is the future employment outlook for entertainment engineers? How is the field changing?

- Entertainment engineering seems like a hard field to enter. What can I do now to prepare for the field?

Reach out to your network (parents, family friends, teachers, etc.) to see if anyone knows an entertainment engineer. If they can't recommend an entertainment engineer, ask if they know an electrical, civil, mechanical, industrial, or other type of engineer. Professional associations, entertainment companies, and entertainment engineering firms can also help arrange an information interview.

TEXT-DEPENDENT QUESTIONS:

1. Why do entertainment engineers need good communication skills?
2. What resources are offered by the Technology Student Association?
3. What is job shadowing?

RESEARCH PROJECT:

Try out at least three of the career exploration suggestions (e.g., job shadowing, competitions, camps) that were discussed in this chapter. What did you learn about entertainment engineering? Write a report and present it to your science class.

WORDS TO UNDERSTAND

application: in the computer industry, software that is designed to perform a function

artificial intelligence: the simulation of human intelligence by machinery and computer systems

prestige: respected and admired

recession: a period of economic decline in one country, several countries, or worldwide, in which many banks fail, the real estate sector crashes, trade declines, and many people lose their jobs

recruiting firm: a company that matches job seekers with job openings

Chapter 5

THE FUTURE OF ENTERTAINMENT ENGINEERING CAREERS

THE BIG PICTURE

There will continue to be job opportunities in the global theme and amusement park industry. From 2019–2021, growth will average an estimated 2.4 percent compounded annually, according to the *2011–2021 Global Theme and Amusement Park Outlook* from the International Association of Amusement Parks and Attractions. It predicts that overall spending in the industry will reach an estimated $56.5 billion in 2021, a 5.6 percent compound annual increase from 2016.

Demand is growing for entertainment engineers throughout the world. Ramayana Water Park in Pattaya, Thailand, is just one example of a recreational facility that was designed by entertainment engineers.

While there are opportunities for highly skilled and talented engineers in the global theme and amusement park industry, it's important to remember that there are only, perhaps, 5,000 to 10,000 people who work full time as entertainment engineers in the world at any given time. This makes getting a job challenging, but not impossible. The most promising job candidates have degrees in more than one engineering discipline, have taken special entertainment engineering courses at colleges and universities and through professional associations, and have completed at least one—but ideally several—internships at entertainment engineering firms. Additionally, job candidates who have excellent communication and interpersonal skills, who are able to effectively use technology (such as CAD software), who are able to work as a member of a team, and who are willing to travel frequently will have the best job prospects. Proficiency (skill) in at least one foreign language will be useful if you want to work for an international entertainment engineering firm.

BARRIERS TO GROWTH IN THE ENTERTAINMENT ENGINEERING INDUSTRY

Although the future of entertainment engineering looks good, there are several issues that may slow growth.

CHALLENGING ECONOMIC TIMES

If another **recession** occurs, there will be less money to spend on building new theme parks, water parks, and other entertainment facilities. There will also be fewer stage productions and fewer television shows and movies that incorporate big-budget visual effects. If this occurs, demand will decrease for entertainment engineers. But even if a recession occurs, there will continue to be opportunities for entertainment engineers to troubleshoot and repair existing systems and structures. Keep in mind that recessions don't last forever. Job opportunities will eventually increase. A recession typically occurs every five years or so, but some recessions are more severe than others and last longer.

RISING MANUFACTURING COSTS

If the cost of steel and other building materials increases significantly, it will be more expensive to build new roller coasters, Ferris wheels, and entire amusement or water parks. If costs rise, some entertainment companies will delay or even cancel major building projects. If this occurs, there will be fewer opportunities in entertainment engineering.

DECLINING PUBLIC INTEREST

If the public loses interest in attending theatrical performances, visiting water parks, riding roller coasters and other rides, and watching special effects in

> If the cost of steel and other raw materials rises, it will be more expensive to build amusement parks, and there may be fewer jobs for entertainment engineers.

movies and television shows, there will be less demand for entertainment engineers. But it would be very surprising if this happened—unless some form of new entertainment emerges that wows the world. The public loves visiting theme parks; taking a break from the cold in an indoor waterpark; and watching stage shows in Las Vegas, New York City, or their hometown. Unless something unpredictable happens, the career of entertainment engineer is here to stay.

WOMEN IN ENGINEERING

Although women comprise approximately 50 percent of the world population, only about 13 percent of engineers are female, but the percentage is higher in certain engineering professions. Here are the most popular engineering degrees earned by females in 2016–2017, according to the Society for Women Engineers:

1. Mechanical
2. Chemical
3. Civil
4. Biomedical
5. Computer science
6. Industrial/manufacturing/systems
7. Electrical
8. Computer engineering
9. Environmental
10. Metallurgical materials

If you're a woman, you should seriously consider a career in engineering. There's no other field that offers so many career options (including

entertainment engineering), great salaries, and many job opportunities. Here are a few organizations that can help you learn more:

- Society of Women Engineers: http://societyofwomenengineers.swe.org
- EngineerGirl: www.engineergirl.org
- IEEE Women in Engineering: www.ieee.org/membership/women-in-engineering.html

ADDITIONAL OPPORTUNITIES IN ENGINEERING

There are many opportunities for women in entertainment engineering.

While it can sometimes be challenging to land a full-time job in entertainment engineering—especially if you've just graduated from college—there is strong demand for engineers in almost every other engineering field. So even if you can't break into the entertainment industry at first, you will be able to find a job as an engineer in another industry. Let's take a look at the employment outlook from the U.S. Department of Labor for a variety of engineering specialties.

MECHANICAL ENGINEERING

Employment of mechanical engineers is expected to increase by 9 percent (or as fast as the average for all occupations) from

Employment opportunities for mechanical engineers are strong in many industries.

2016 to 2026. Mechanical engineers who work in engineering services (including those that provide services to the entertainment industry) will have especially strong prospects as companies continue to contract work from these firms. There are also many jobs because mechanical engineers have a broad skill set that allows them to find opportunities in many industries.

The USDL reports that opportunities for mechanical engineers "will be best for those with training in the latest software tools, particularly for computational design and simulation. Such tools allow engineers and designers to take a project from the conceptual phase directly to a finished product, eliminating the need for prototypes. Engineers who have experience or training in three-dimensional printing also will have better job prospects."

A few years back, the American Society of Mechanical Engineers (ASME) conducted a survey of more than 1,200 engineers who had a minimum of two years of experience in mechanical engineering–related positions. According to an ASME report, which gathered information from that survey and other sources, the association made the following quoted predictions:

- The **prestige** of working as an engineer will increase

- The financial rewards of working as an engineer will be greater

- The number of engineers working in less-developed countries will be greater

- The need for engineers to increase their ability to communicate more effectively, increase language skills, and manage global teams will increase

- Skills in motion simulation, animation, and virtual prototype creation are needed

Demand for mechanical engineers is also strong outside the United States. The **recruiting firm** Michael Page reports that there is a shortage of mechanical engineers in nearly twenty countries, including Canada, Mexico, Ireland, Germany, Australia, New Zealand, and the United Kingdom.

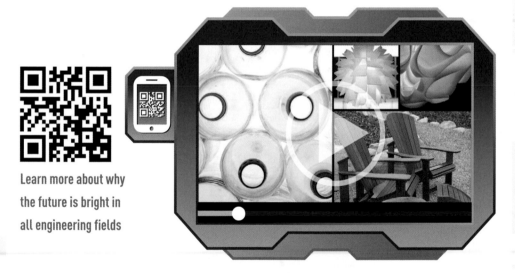

Learn more about why the future is bright in all engineering fields

CIVIL ENGINEERING

Job opportunities for civil engineers are projected to grow by 11 percent from 2016 to 2026. The USDL says that "new standards known collectively as the Body of Knowledge are growing in importance within civil engineering, and this development is likely to result in a heightened need for a graduate education.

Therefore those who enter the occupation with a graduate degree will likely have better prospects."

Outside the United States, the recruiting firm Michael Page reports that there is a shortage of civil engineers in more than fifteen countries, including the United Kingdom, Spain, Russia, Canada, Mexico, Brazil, Australia, and New Zealand.

DAY IN THE LIFE: WATERSLIDE ENGINEER

When I tell people what I do, people always say that I have the greatest job—and I do! Not every career is associated with fun and good memories, but mine is.

I've worked as a waterslide designer and engineer for about seven years. To prepare for the field, I earned degrees in both mechanical and structural engineering and took specialized classes in entertainment engineering. I also rode tons of waterslides—and still do—to learn what users like and dislike about their experiences.

We use CAD software to design each waterslide. The software allows us to simulate the actual use of the waterslide. We see where each user would travel within the waterslide during their experience, which allows us to address safety issues and make the ride as exciting and rewarding as possible. An example of a safety issue that we identify before construction might involve realizing that we did not include enough space in the straightaways. This situation might cause riders to move too quickly and launch off the slide, creating a dangerous situation.

That's just one example of a typical challenge that I encounter on the job. Some people might not like to work in a career that involves constant problem-solving, but I do. This is a rewarding field. You're not stuck in an office all day. You get to spend a lot of time outdoors or at indoor water parks. And you get to test the waterslides dozens of times until they're ready for the public. Flying down a waterslide is certainly not part of the job description of any other career! If you want an exciting career that allows you to use both your science and engineering skills and your creativity, you should consider becoming an entertainment engineer.

ENVIRONMENTAL ENGINEERING

Employment for environmental engineers will increase by 8 percent from 2016 to 2026. Outside the entertainment industry, there will be strong demand for environmental engineers by the government at all levels and by companies (especially in the utility and energy industries) that need assistance with wastewater treatment issues. Those with a master's degree in environmental engineering will have the best prospects. Opportunities for environmental engineers are also growing because many engineers are expected to retire in the next decade.

ELECTRICAL AND ELECTRONICS ENGINEERING

Job prospects for electrical and electronics engineers are expected to increase by 7 percent from 2016 to 2026. The USDL reports that the strongest growth will be in engineering services firms (including those that provide services to the entertainment industry) "as more companies are expected to tap the expertise of engineers in this industry for projects involving electronic devices and systems. The rapid pace of technological innovation will likely drive demand for electrical and electronics engineers in research and development, an area in which engineering expertise will be needed to design distribution systems related to new technologies."

INDUSTRIAL ENGINEERING

Employment of industrial engineers is expected to increase by 10 percent from 2016 to 2026, faster than the average for all careers. Industrial engineers have a wide range of skills that allow them to work in many fields. Since every company, organization, and government agency is interested in improving efficiency, there's always a need for industrial engineers.

The USDL says that engineers with knowledge of manufacturing engineering may find better prospects for employment. Outside of the United States, the recruiting firm Michael Page reports that there is a shortage of industrial engineers in Belgium, Germany, Chile, Canada, New Zealand, and Australia.

SOFTWARE ENGINEERING

Software is used in nearly every area of life these days, including entertainment engineering. As a result, there is very strong demand for software engineers. In fact, employment of software engineers (who are sometimes known as software developers) is projected to increase by 24 percent from 2016 to 2026, which is much faster than the average for all careers. Outside the entertainment industry, there will be strong demand for software engineers in smartphone and tablet **application** development, in the health and medical insurance industries, and in the field of cybersecurity. The USDL says that "prospects will be best for applicants with knowledge of the most up-to-date programming tools and for those who are proficient in one or more programming languages."

TECHNOLOGY AND THE FUTURE OF ENTERTAINMENT ENGINEERING

The fields of entertainment engineering (and engineering in general) have changed immensely because of advances in technology. For example, helicopters and airplanes were used in the past to collect information about potential construction sites or ongoing projects. Their use was expensive and time consuming. Today, drones that cost as little as $50 are used to quickly gather information. They're also being used in the staging of entertainment shows.

Here are a few other ways technology will change the industry:

- CAD programs will continue to become more complex and allow engineers to create more detailed designs in less time than in the past.

Increasingly, 3-D printing technology is expected to be incorporated into a variety of entertainment systems.

- 3-D printing technology will be increasingly used onsite to create new or replacement parts for systems and structures.

- The computing power of data analytics software combined with **artificial intelligence** will allow engineering firms to collect and analyze large amounts of data that will help them work more efficiently. "Digitization is changing the playing field for engineers," according to *Industry Week*. "It alters the culture by providing more real-time data on the performance of equipment in the field today, allowing engineers to consider improvements that can be achieved in months through data algorithms rather than years or decades."

- New building materials will be developed that will allow engineers to create larger, faster, and more complex amusement park rides, water park features, and other entertainment systems and structures.

Despite advances in technology (which may eliminate some basic tasks for engineers), engineering is one field that will never go away. "Engineers exist to solve problems," advises the Redline Group, a European technology recruiting

There will continue to be good opportunities for entertainment engineers because amusement parks, water parks, and other entertainment venues remain very popular with the public.

firm. "That need is never going to go away. Technology is transforming the way in which we work, think and live, and engineers will be at the forefront of these changes, transforming the digital age in everything from manufacturing to robotics."

IN CLOSING

Can you see yourself designing the fastest or tallest roller coaster in the world? How about a massive stage for the next Taylor Swift or Chance the Rapper concert? Are you creative, do you like to solve problems, and do you have good technical and design skills? Are you looking for a career that offers good pay and steady job prospects? If so, then a career as an entertainment engineer could be in your future.

I hope that you'll use this book as a starting point to discover even more about careers in this field. Talk to entertainment engineers about their careers and shadow them on the job, use the resources of professional organizations, and, most importantly, start designing and building things (e.g., Ferris wheels, mini-stages, lighting systems, etc.) to develop your skills. Good luck on your career exploration!

TEXT-DEPENDENT QUESTIONS:

1. Why is the employment outlook good for entertainment engineers?
2. What developments might slow growth in entertainment engineering?
3. What is a recession?

RESEARCH PROJECT:

Spend some time exploring how the entertainment engineering industry will change in the future. How will these changes affect the necessary educational and skill requirements for future engineers? Write a report about your findings and present it to your class.

PHOTO CREDITS

6: Digikhmer | Dreamstime.com
10: Valeo5 | Dreamstime.com
14: Goodluz | Dreamstime.com
15: Byelikova | Dreamstime.com
16: Waihs | Dreamstime.com
19: Chrisstanley | Dreamstime.com
21: Ritu Jethani | Dreamstime.com
25: Milotus | Dreamstime.com
28: Ilya Platonov | Dreamstime.com
30: Shutterbox | Dreamstime.com
32: Marek Uliasz | Dreamstime.com
36–37: Luckyphotographer |
    Dreamstime.com
38: Photomall | Dreamstime.com
40: Skolton | Dreamstime.com
42: Monkey Business Images |
    Dreamstime.com
45: Monkey Business Images |
    Shutterstock
46: Monkey Business Images |
    Shutterstock
48: Navy Seaman Christopher A.
    Michaels | U.S. Department of
    Defense
50: Vadim Orlov | Dreamstime.com

56: Kobby Dagan | Dreamstime.com
60: Thakkura Podjanapon |
    Dreamstime.com
62: thanmano | Shutterstock
64: Feblacal | Dreamstime.com
71: Igor Akimov | Dreamstime.com
72: U.S. Department of Defense
73: Monkey Business Images |
    Shutterstock
75: sirtravelalot | Shutterstock
78: Berniephillips | Dreamstime.com
80: Supawat Chuenchoosap |
    Dreamstime.com
82: Igor Akimov | Dreamstime.com
83: Nyul | Dreamstime.com
84: Vladimir Grigorev | Dreamstime.
    com
89: Tixtis | Dreamstime.com
90: Syda Productions | Shutterstock

Cover Photos: © GOLFX | Shutterstock

FURTHER READING

Baine, Celeste. *Is There an Engineer Inside You?: A Comprehensive Guide to Career Decisions in Engineering.* 5th ed. Clarkesville, Ga.: Engineering Education Service Center, 2016.

Brain, Marshall. *The Engineering Book: From the Catapult to the Curiosity Rover, 250 Milestones in the History of Engineering.* New York: Sterling, 2015.

Graves, Colleen, and Aaron Graves. *The Big Book of Makerspace Projects: Inspiring Makers to Experiment, Create, and Learn.* New York: McGraw-Hill Education, 2016.

Greer, Paul. *STEM Careers: A Student's Guide to Opportunities in Science, Technology, Engineering and Maths.* Bath, United Kingdom: Trotman Education, 2018.

INTERNET RESOURCES

www.unlv.edu/sites/default/files/assets/advising/pdf/CareerGuide-EntertainmentEngineeringDesign-Engineering.pdf:
This website provides more information on the University of Nevada at Las Vegas' entertainment engineering and design program, career resources, and salaries in the field.

www.nacme.org/publications/middle_and_highschool/NACME_ESA_HS_MagENG.pdf:
Engineer Something Amazing!—Why You Should Consider Earning a Degree in Engineering is a twelve-page brochure from the National Action Council for Minorities in Engineering that provides a wealth of information on the types of engineers, preparing for the field, and things you can do while in school to learn more about engineering.

www.bls.gov/ooh/architecture-and-engineering/home.htm:
This section of the *Occupational Outlook Handbook* features information on job duties, educational requirements, salaries, and the employment outlook for more than thirty careers in engineering and architecture.

www.egfi-k12.org/index_noflash.php:
This resource from the American Society for Engineering Education provides information on more than fifteen engineering careers and features profiles of people in these careers.

INDEX

INDEX

EDUCATIONAL VIDEO LINKS

Chapter 1:
An entertainment engineer who earned an engineering degree from the University of Kentucky discusses his career: http://x-qr.net/1Jyb

A roller coaster engineer explains why he loves his career: http://x-qr.net/1M5Z

A theme park engineer at Walt Disney discusses her career and the key traits and educational preparation needed for engineers in this specialty: http://x-qr.net/1KHs

Chapter 3:
Learn how students at Purdue University use virtual reality to design roller coasters: http://x-qr.net/1M44

Chapter 4:
Watch a group of high school students participate in the Marshmallow Challenge, a competition that helps them to develop their design and engineering skills: http://x-qr.net/1L2K

Chapter 5:
Learn more about why the future is bright in all engineering fields: http://x-qr.net/1KoJ

AUTHOR BIOGRAPHY

Andrew Morkes has been a writer and editor for more than twenty-five years. He is the author of more than twenty-five books about college-planning and careers, including all of the titles in this series, many titles in the Careers in the Building Trades series, the *Vault Career Guide to Social Media*, and *They Teach That in College!?: A Resource Guide to More Than 100 Interesting College Majors*, which was selected as one of the best books of the year by the library journal *Voice of Youth Advocates*. He is also the author and publisher of "The Morkes Report: College and Career Planning Trends" blog.